Cutting Activities

M000094057

Written by Sue Lambert and Sandi Rickerby

Published by World Teachers Press®

Published with the permission of R.I.C. Publications Pty. Ltd.

Copyright © 1999 by Didax, Inc., Rowley, MA 01969. All rights reserved.

First published by R.I.C. Publications Pty. Ltd., Perth, Western Australia.

Limited reproduction permission: The publisher grants permission to individual teachers who have purchased this book to reproduce the blackline masters as needed for use with their own students. Reproduction for an entire school or school district or for commercial use is prohibited.

Printed in the United States of America.

Order Number 2-5101
ISBN 1-58324-023-3

G H I J K 09 08 07 06 05

Didax
Educational Resources

395 Main Street
Rowley, MA 01969
www.worldteacherspress.com

Foreword

The *Early Skills Series* of books is designed to give students practice in a range of early reading, writing and number activities as well as developing perceptual and fine motor skills in the early years.

Early Skills Series – Cutting Activities provides students with the opportunity to practice their fine motor skills as well as early perceptual skills in the area of space. Using this book students will complete activities such as making jigsaw puzzles, drawing symmetrical shapes and constructing given pictures. These can then be pasted into the frame on page 47, or onto a blank sheet of paper.

The worksheets can be used to motivate students to work independently, increase their concentration span and develop their ability to work in an orderly fashion; encouraging them to take pride in the presentation of their work at the same time.

The worksheets are bold, uncluttered and visually appealing to young students. They contain instruction in graphic form, thereby requiring minimum support from the teacher. They can be used to teach a new skill or to reinforce and consolidate those already taught.

Other books in this series are: *Early Skills Series – Counting and Recognition to Five*
Early Skills Series – Addition to Five
Early Skills Series – Early Visual Skills

Contents

Teacher Information

Introduction

Development of perceptual and fine motor skills in the early years is extremely important if students are to have a good grounding to progress to the next level of development. The *Early Skills Series* is designed to give practice in the aforementioned areas in a range of early reading, writing and numerical areas of the curriculum.

The worksheets are motivational and designed to encourage students to work independently wherever possible. This encourages high self-esteem, increases concentration span and develops the ability to work in a logical and orderly fashion.

The clear layout of each worksheet allows the student to concentrate solely on the task at hand. The large, open artwork appeals to students and has been drawn at the appropriate level for students' fine motor skill development.

Suggested Implementation

The *Early Skills Series* can be implemented easily into any existing program.

1. Familiarize students with the icons on page 6. This page could be enlarged and colored and displayed in a prominent position within the classroom. Students can then refer to the icons whenever they need to.
2. Develop recognition and understanding of the key words shown on the worksheets. Students may learn to read these words as sight words. Completing this will help develop their independence in completing the worksheet.
3. Discuss and explain each worksheet after all students have their worksheet in front of them.
   - (a) Students sit on the mat area. You have an enlarged version of the worksheet.
   - (b) Discuss the icons at the top of the page. Students can offer you the instructions for the page.
   - (c) Work through the page, showing the students the completed product.
   - (d) Students move back to their own work area to complete the worksheet independently.
4. Worksheets can be collected and viewed to determine areas of need for each student or the whole class group.

Teacher Information

Instructions

The instructions provided on each worksheet are in graphic form, thereby requiring minimal support from you. A key, explaining each graphic, is located on page 6.

Benefits

The benefits of the *Early Skills Series* are many.

1. You can readily evaluate where each student is having success or difficulty.
2. Students are provided with the opportunity to work independently.
3. Children develop perceptual and fine motor skills in the areas of early reading, writing and numbers.
4. Students become familiar with a general range of instructional text.
5. Students are able to develop logic and work in an orderly fashion.
6. The worksheets are highly motivational.
7. The program is easy to implement into any classroom.

Conclusion

The *Early Skills Series* provides worksheets to cover *Early Visual Skills*, *Cutting*, *Counting and Recognition to Five* and *Addition to Five*; areas which are of major significance in the students' development in the early years of education. A solid grounding in these areas ensures smooth progression onto the next level of development. The activities are designed to allow the students to experience success, developing confidence and a positive self-image toward themselves as a learner.

Key-Cutting Activities

cut
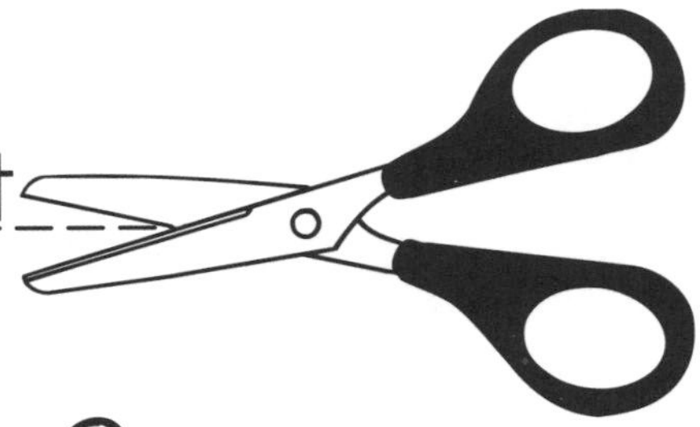

Cut along dotted lines.

glue

Glue the picture in the correct place.

color
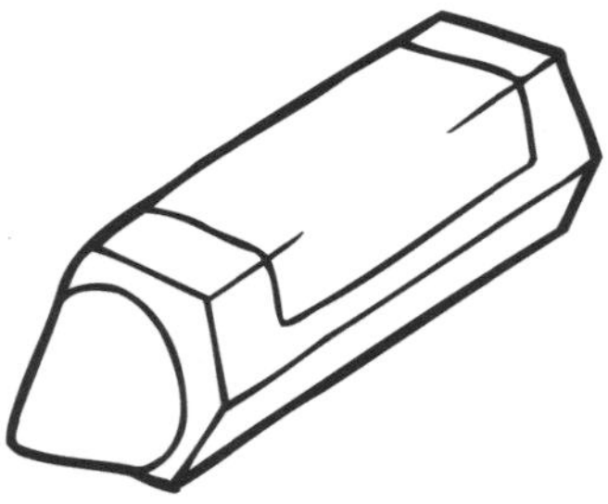

Color the pictures.

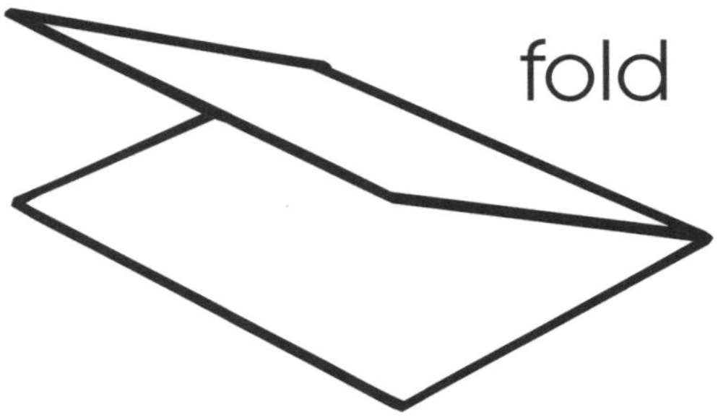
fold

Fold along the straight line.

draw

Draw or finish the picture as shown.

www.worldteacherspress.com © World Teachers Press®

Name: ______________________________ Date: __________________

1. 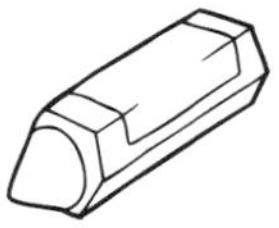 color

2. cut 

3.  glue

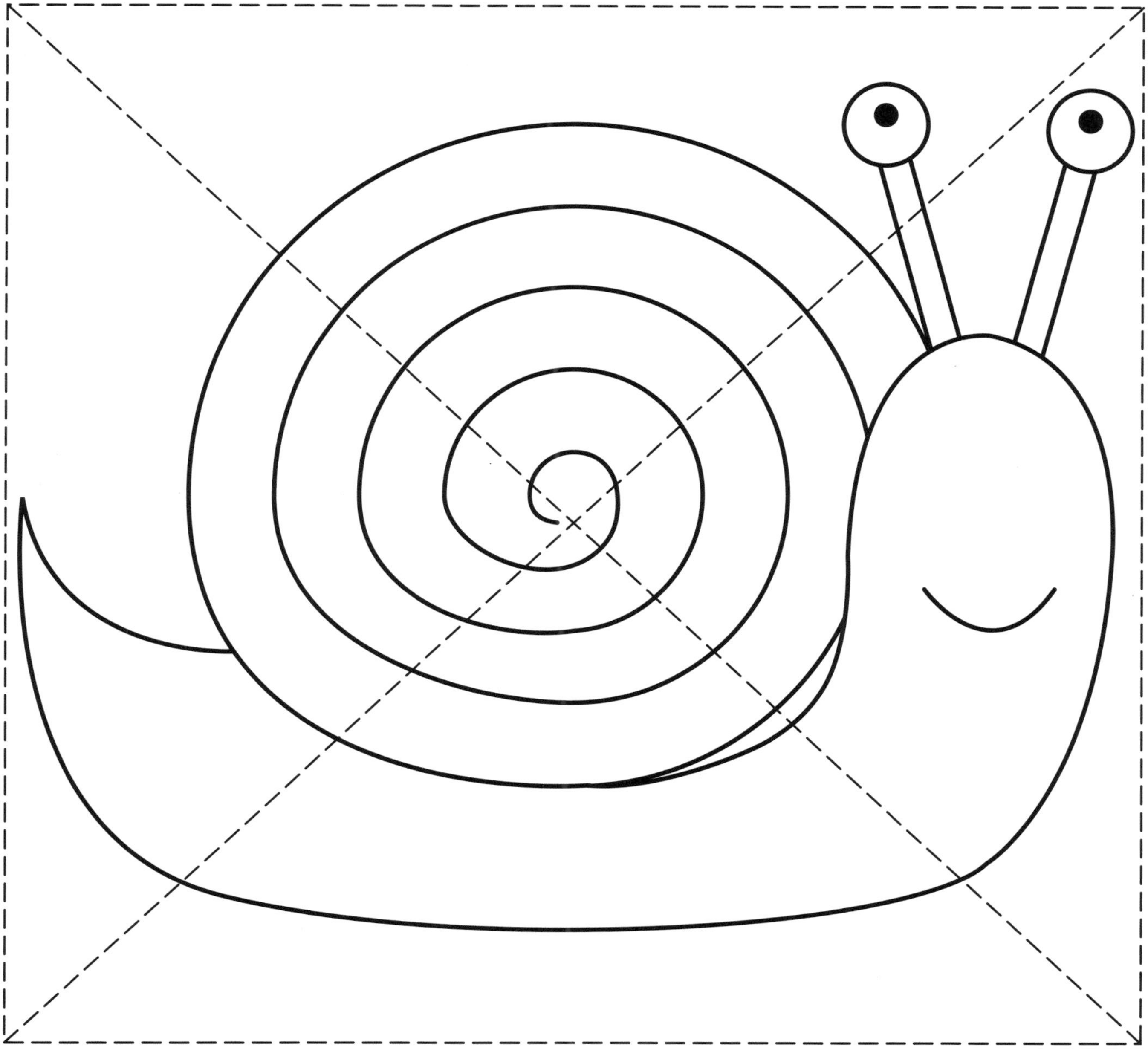

Name: ______________________________ Date: __________________

1. 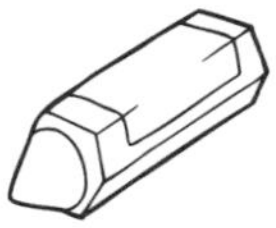 color

2. cut 

3.  glue

Name: ______________________________ Date: __________________

1. 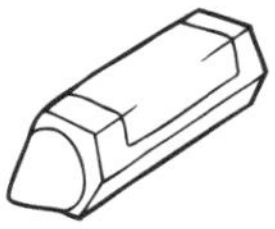 color 2. cut  3.  glue

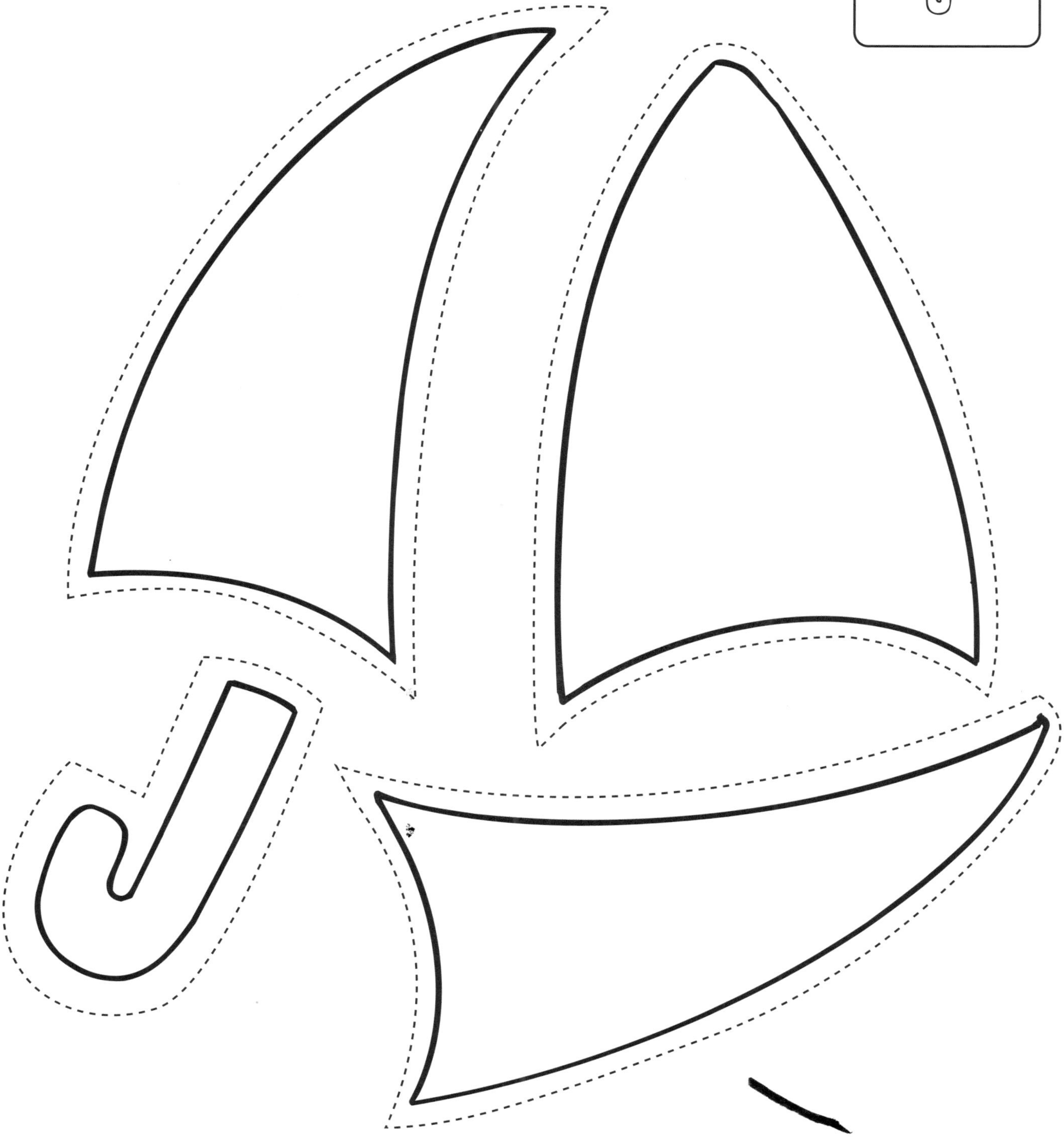

Name: ______________________________ Date: ____________________

1. cut  **2.**  glue **3.** 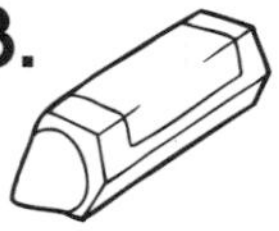 color

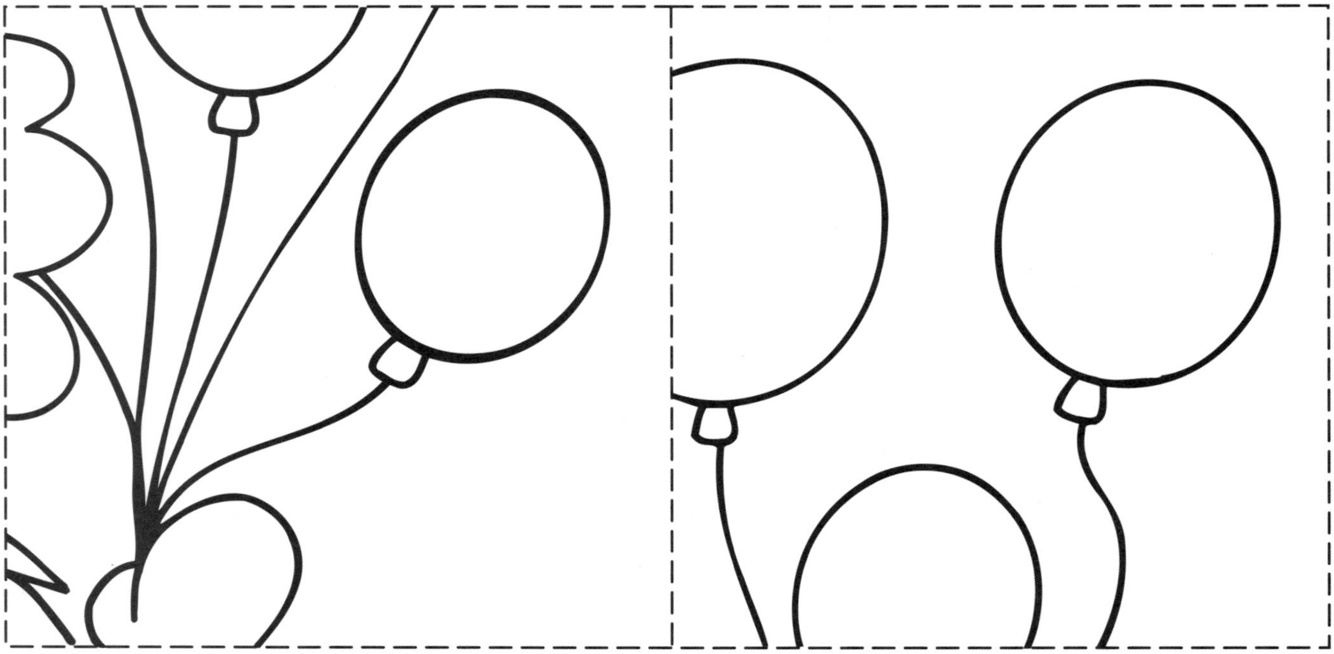

Name: ______________________ Date: ______________

1. cut  2.  glue 3. 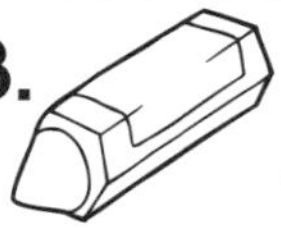 color

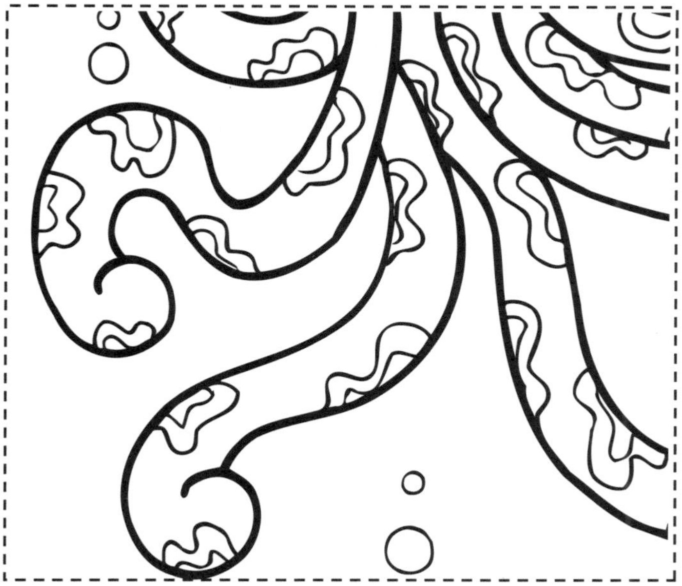

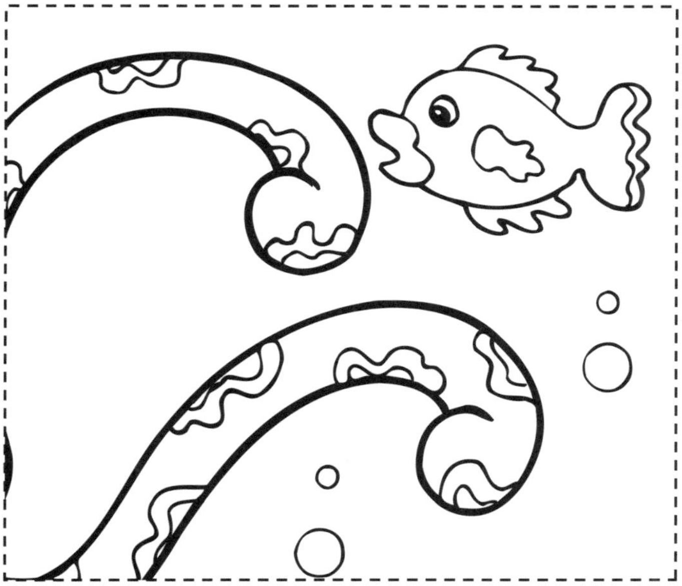

Name: ______________________________ Date: ________________

1. color **2.** cut **3.** glue

Name: ______________________ Date: ______________

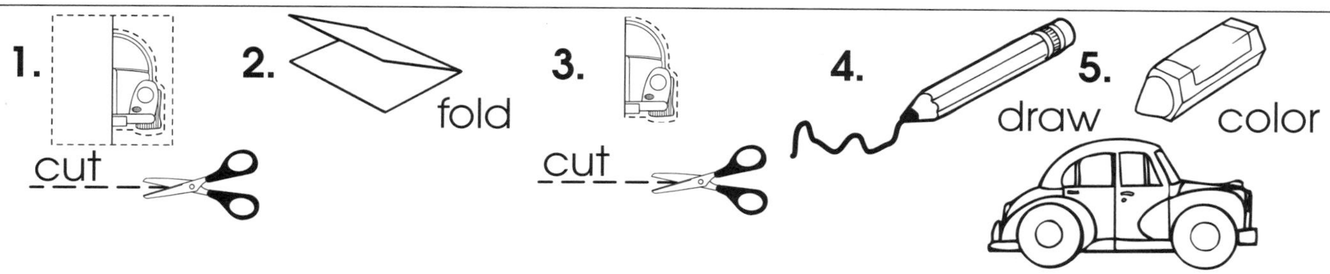

Name: ______________________________ Date: ____________________

1. 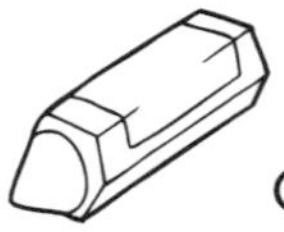 color **2.** cut  **3.**  glue

Name: ______________________ Date: ______________

1. 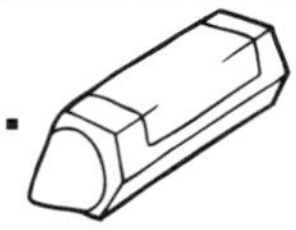 color **2.** cut  **3.**  glue

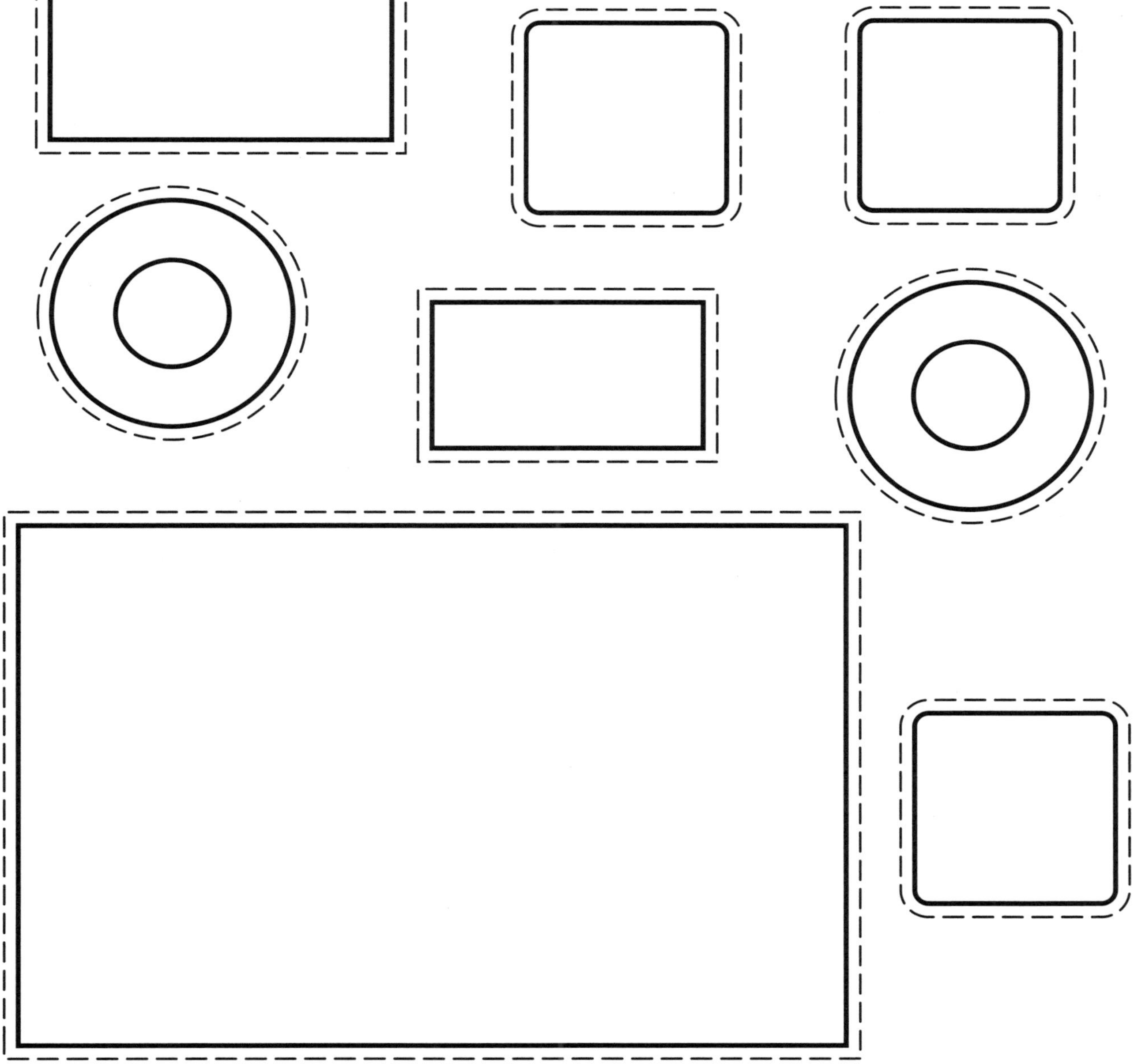

Name: ______________________ Date: ______________

1. 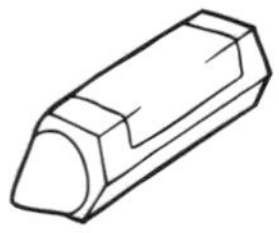 color

2. cut 

3.  glue

 www.worldteacherspress.com © World Teachers Press®

Name: ______________________ Date: ______________

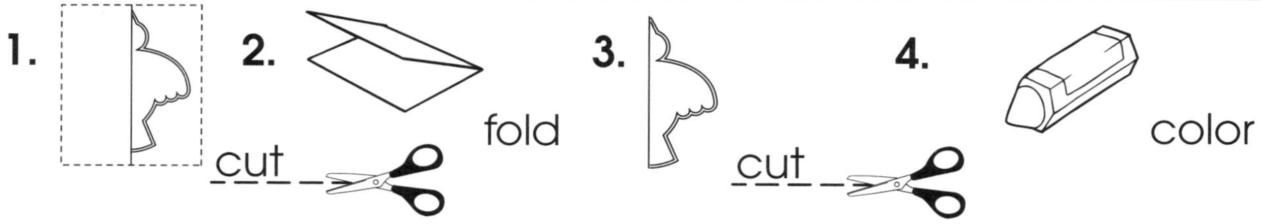

Name: ______________________ Date: ______________

1. 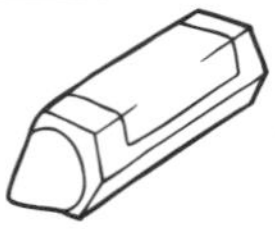 color **2.** cut  **3.**  glue

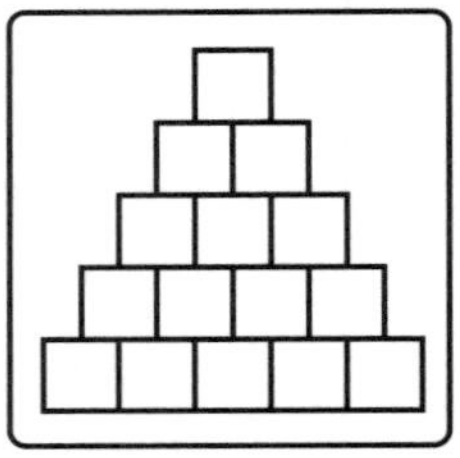

 www.worldteacherspress.com © World Teachers Press®

Name: ______________________________ Date: ____________________

1. cut  **2.**  glue **3.** 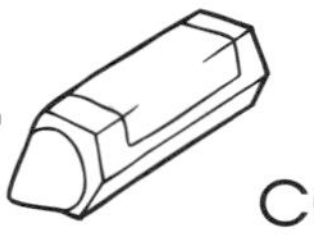 color 

Name: ______________________ Date: ______________

1. 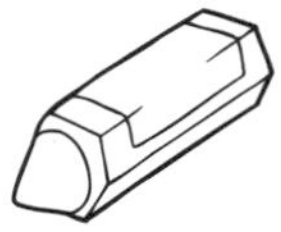 color

2. cut 

3.  glue

 © World Teachers Press®

Name: ______________________________ Date: ____________________

1. 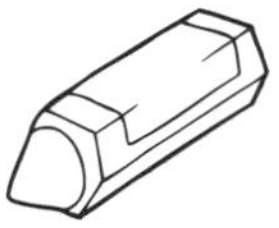 color

2. cut 

3.  glue

Name: ______________________ Date: ______________

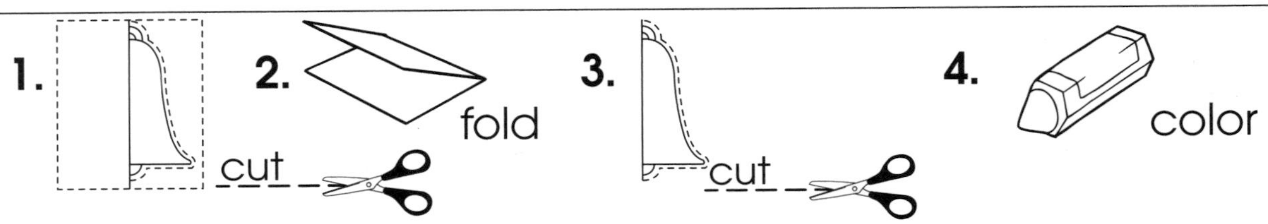

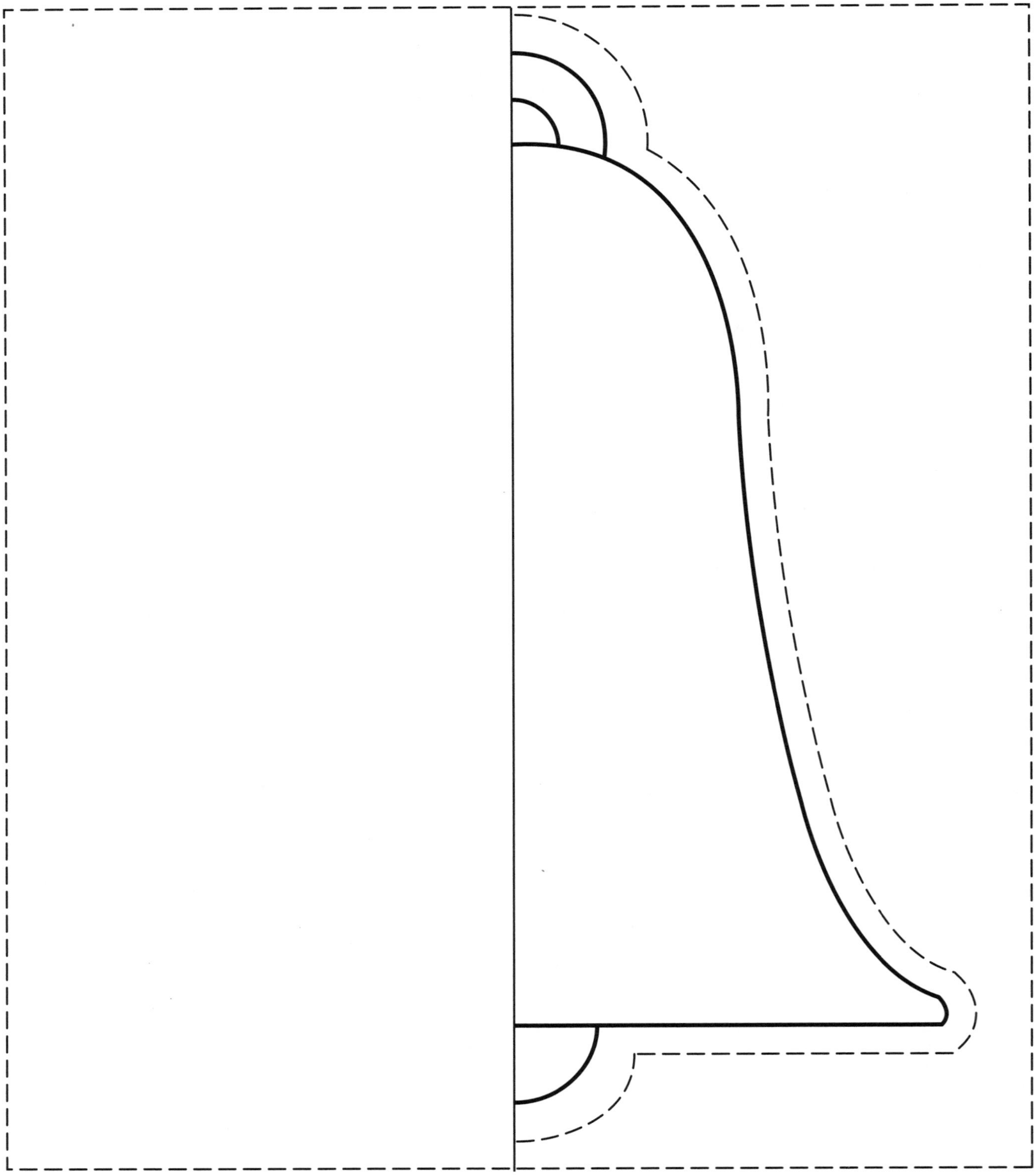

Name: ______________________________ Date: ____________________

1. 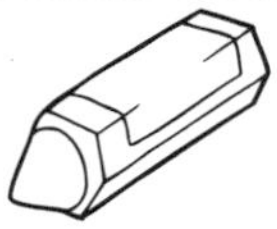 color **2.** cut  **3.**  glue

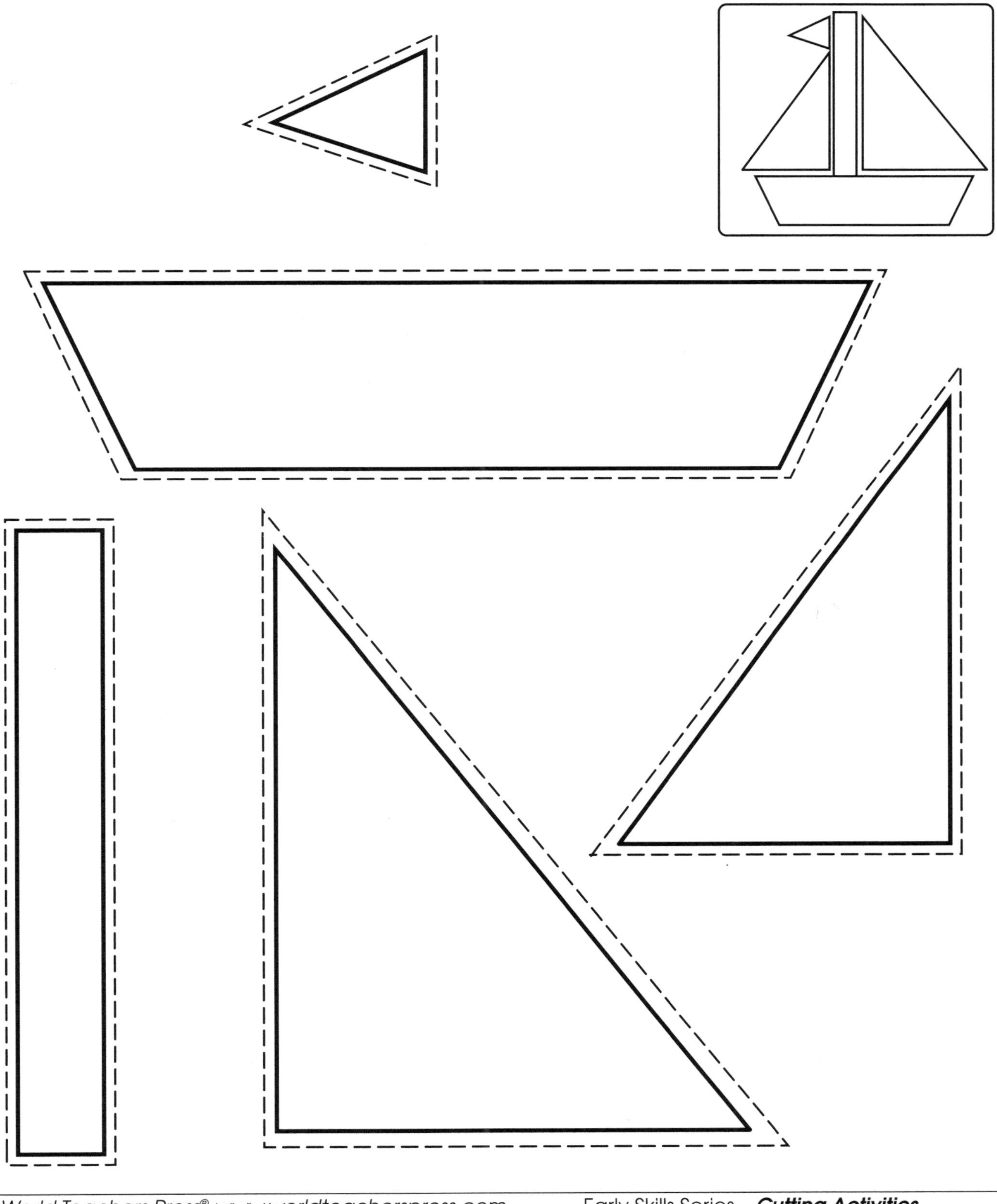

Name: ______________________ Date: ______________

1. 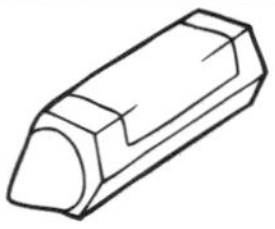 color **2.** cut  **3.**  glue

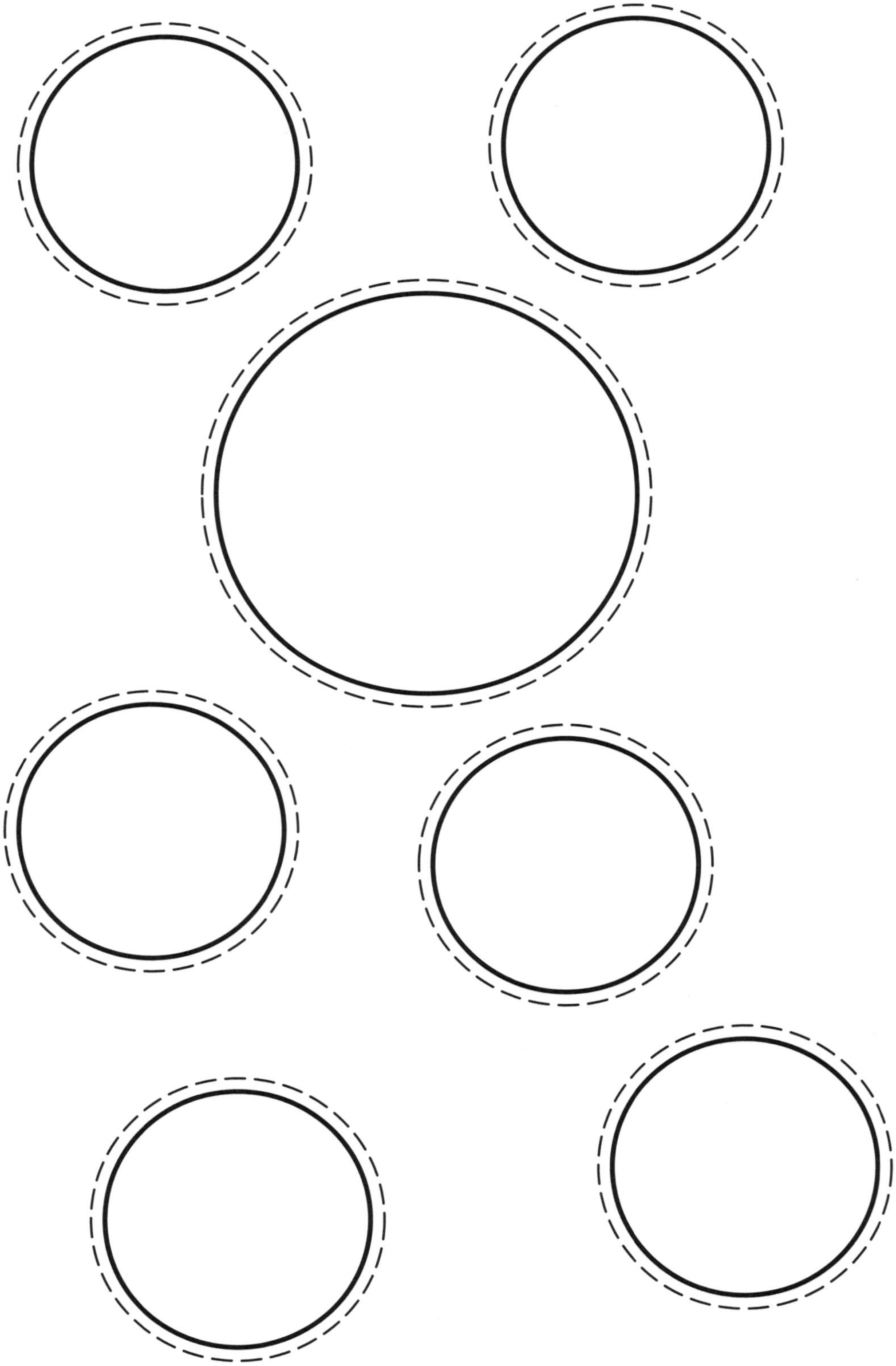

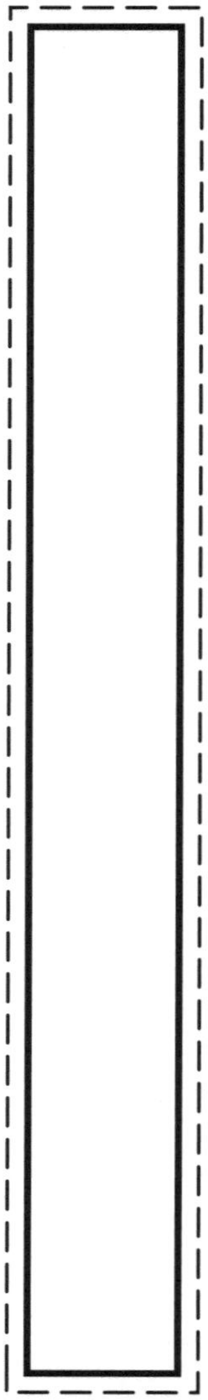

 www.worldteacherspress.com © World Teachers Press®

Name: ______________________ Date: ______________

1. 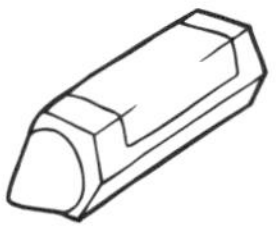 color **2.** cut  **3.**  glue 

Name: ______________________________ Date: ____________________

1. 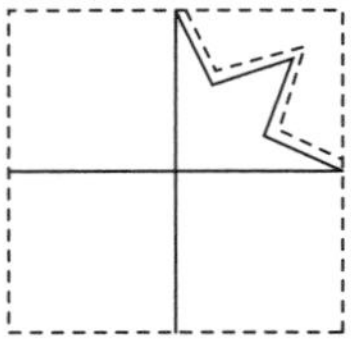 cut 

2. 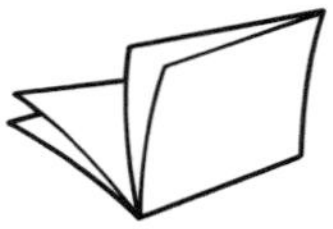 fold

3. 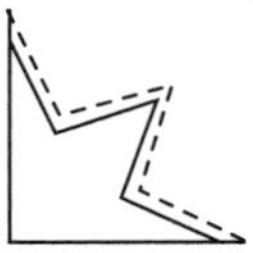 cut 

4. 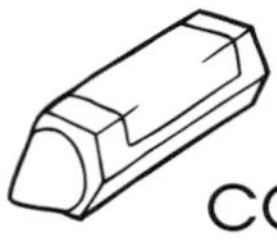 color

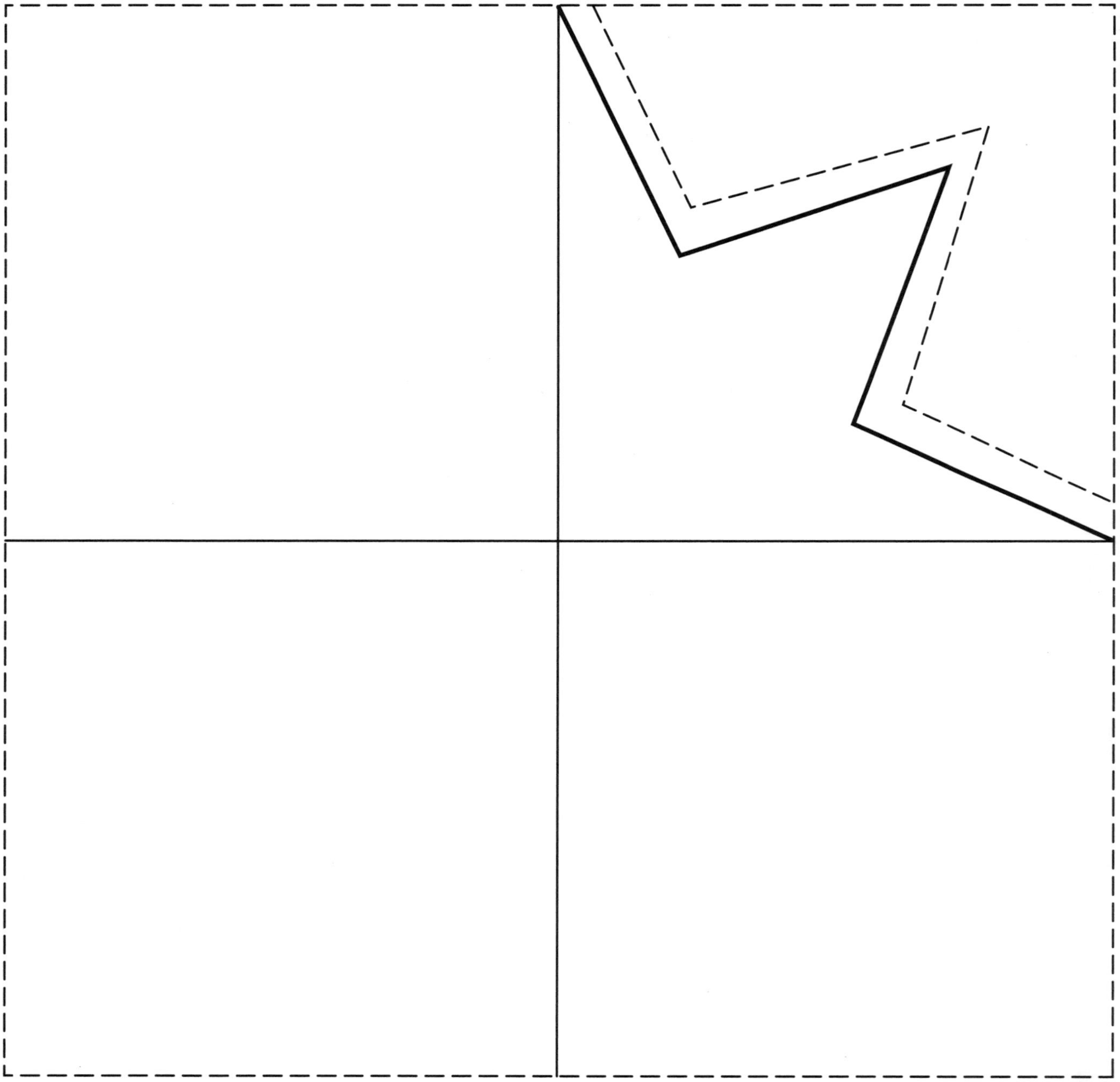

Name: ______________________ Date: ______________

1. color 2. cut 3. glue 4. draw

Name: ______________________ Date: ______________

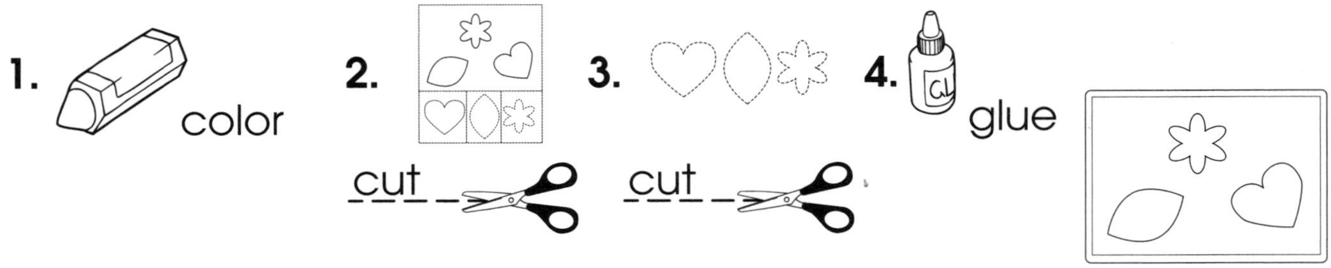

 www.worldteacherspress.com © World Teachers Press®

Name: ______________________________ Date: ____________________

1.  color

2. 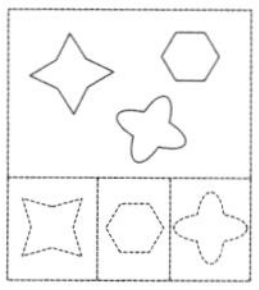

cut 

3. 

cut 

4.  glue 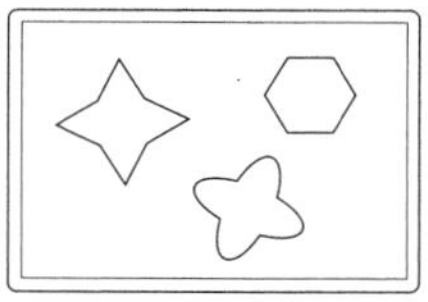

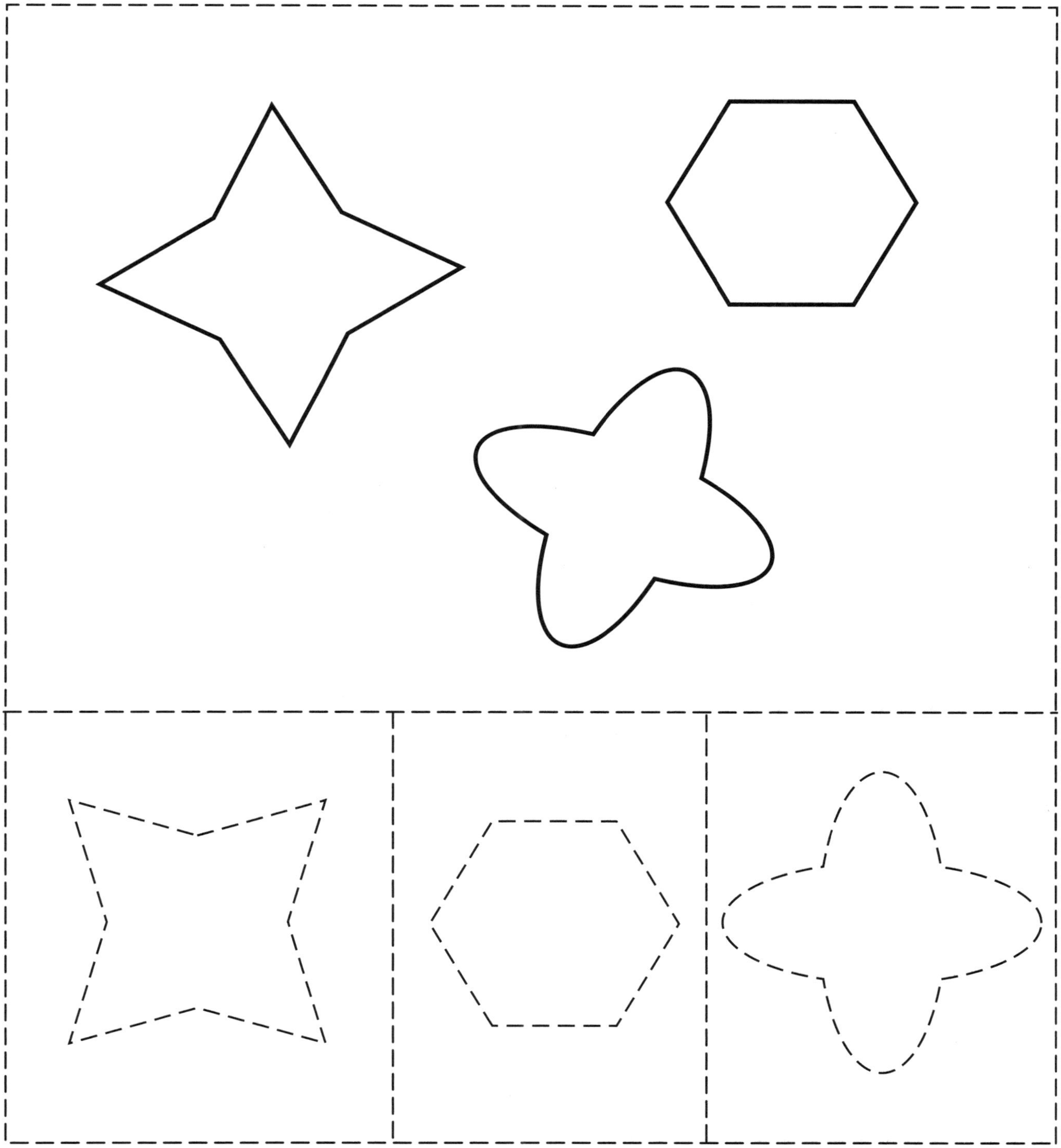

Name: ______________________________ Date: ____________________

1. 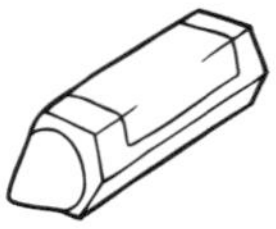 color **2.** cut 

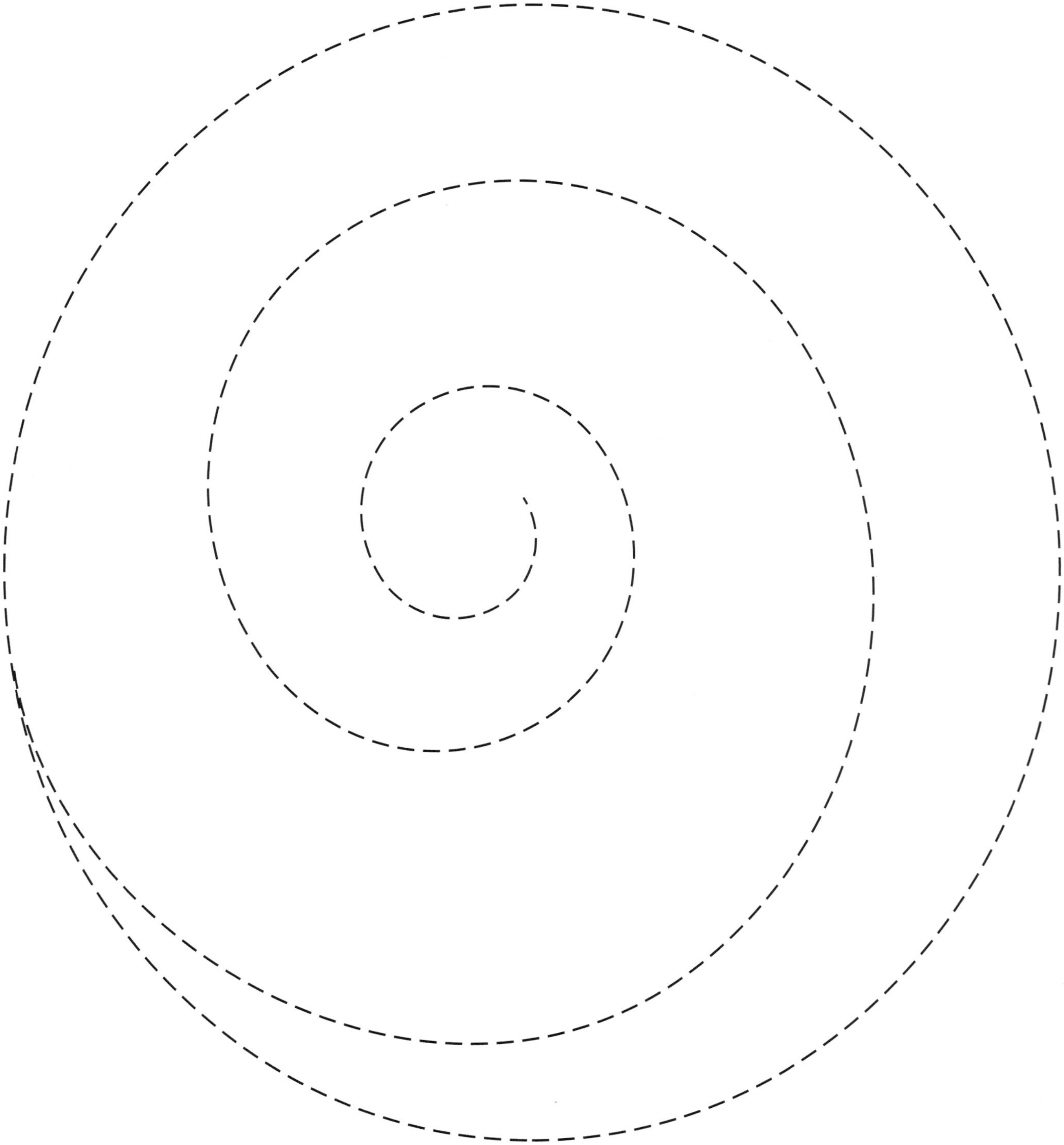

Name: ______________________ Date: ______________

1. 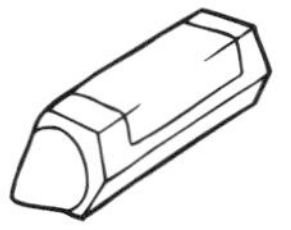 color **2.** cut  **3.**  glue

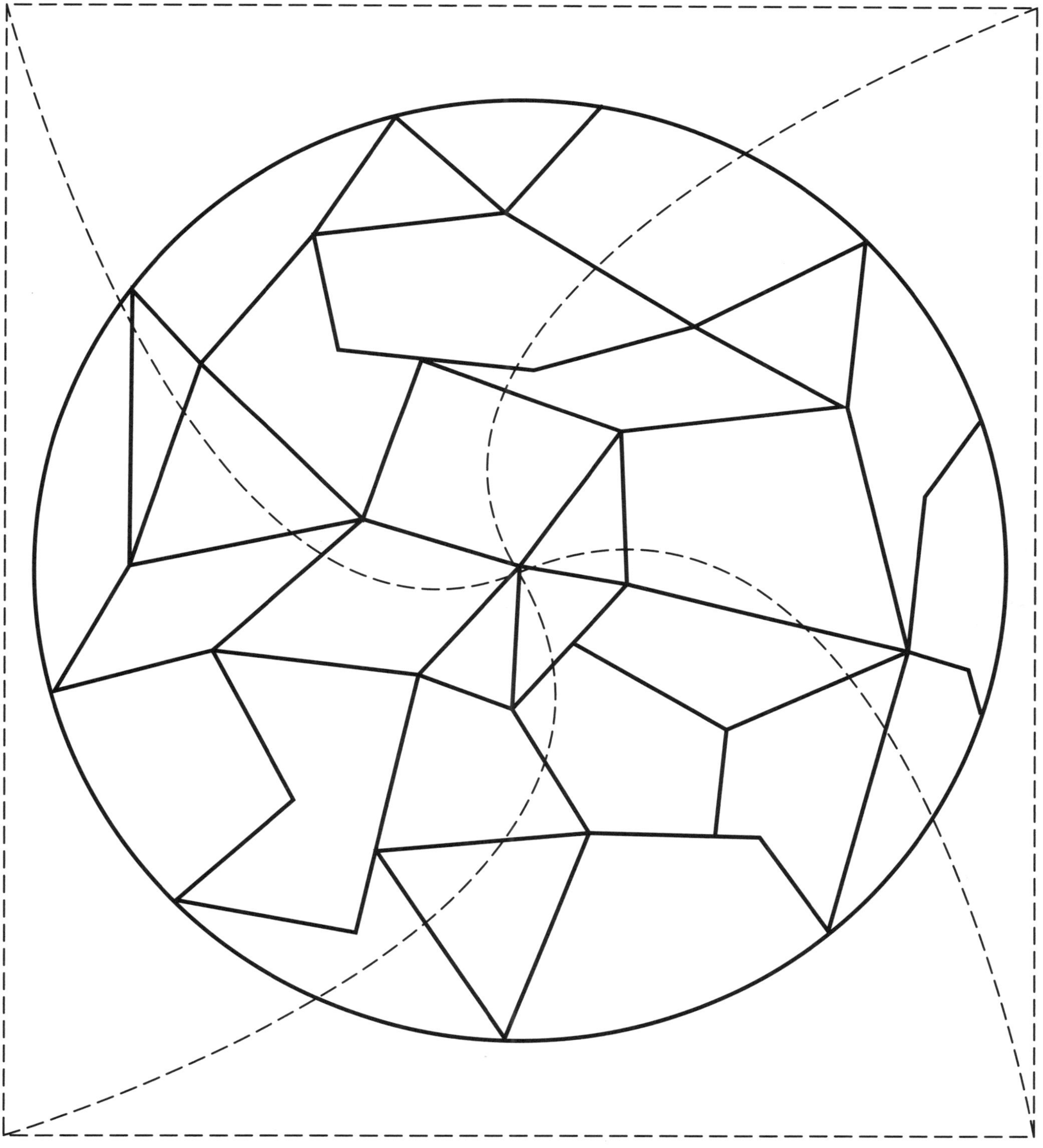

Name: ______________________________ Date: __________________

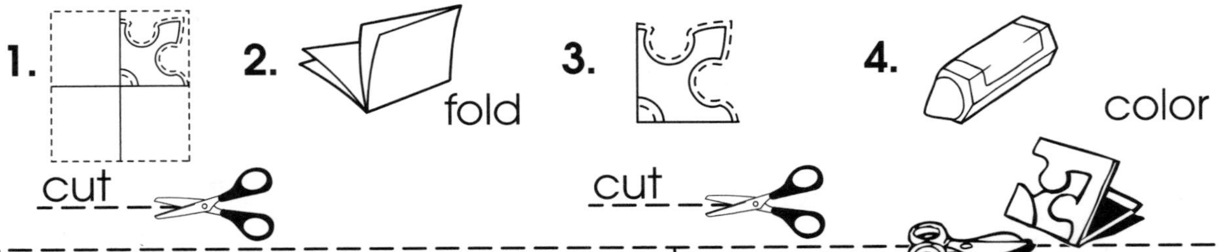

Name: ______________________ Date: ______________

1. 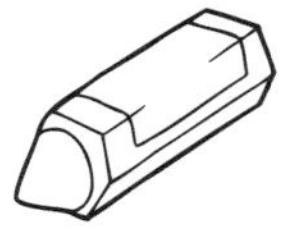 color **2.** cut  **3.**  glue

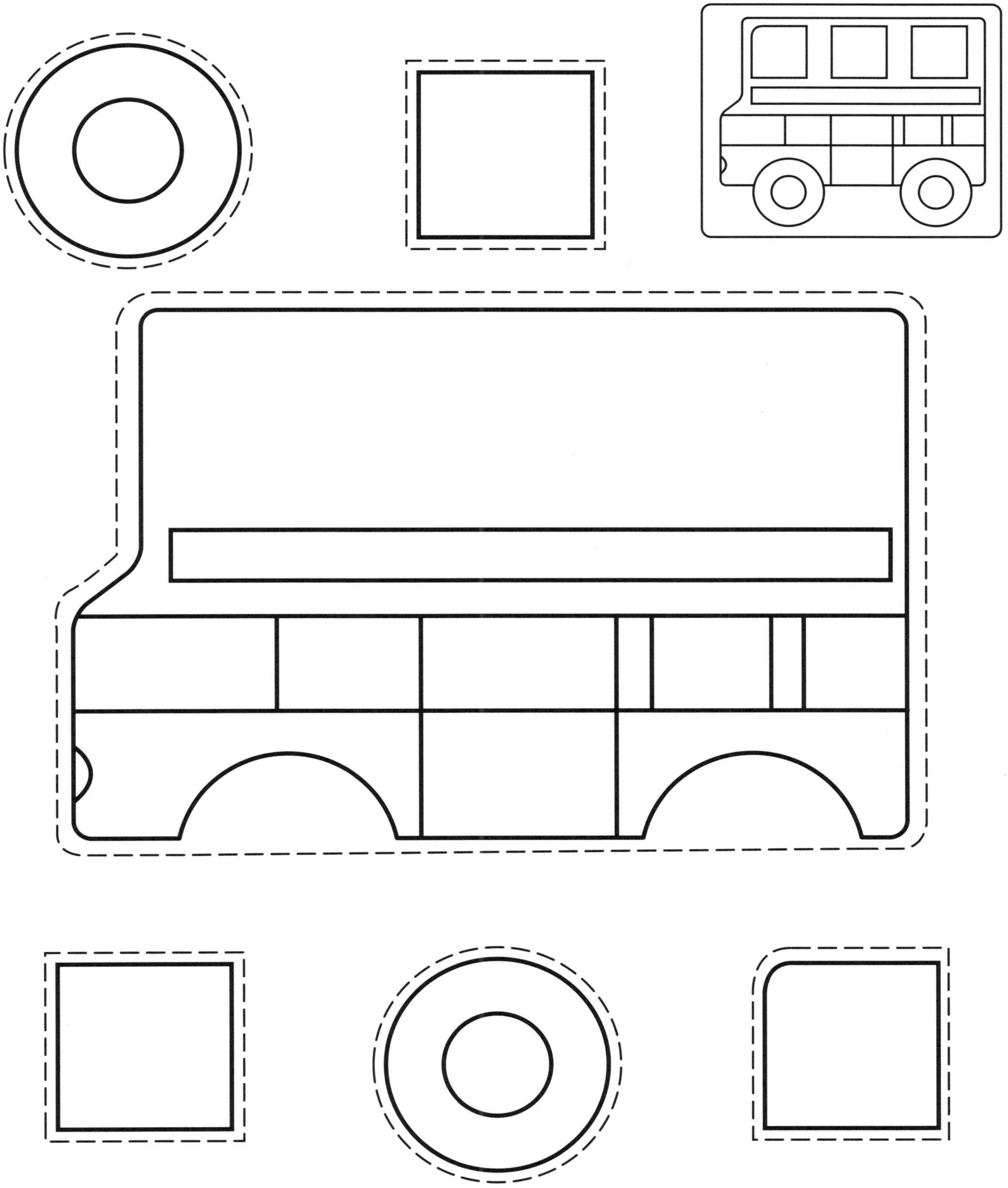

Name: ______________________ Date: ______________

1. cut  **2.**  glue **3.** 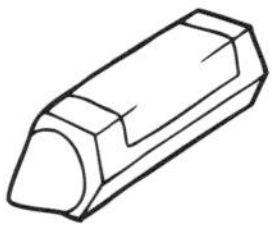 color

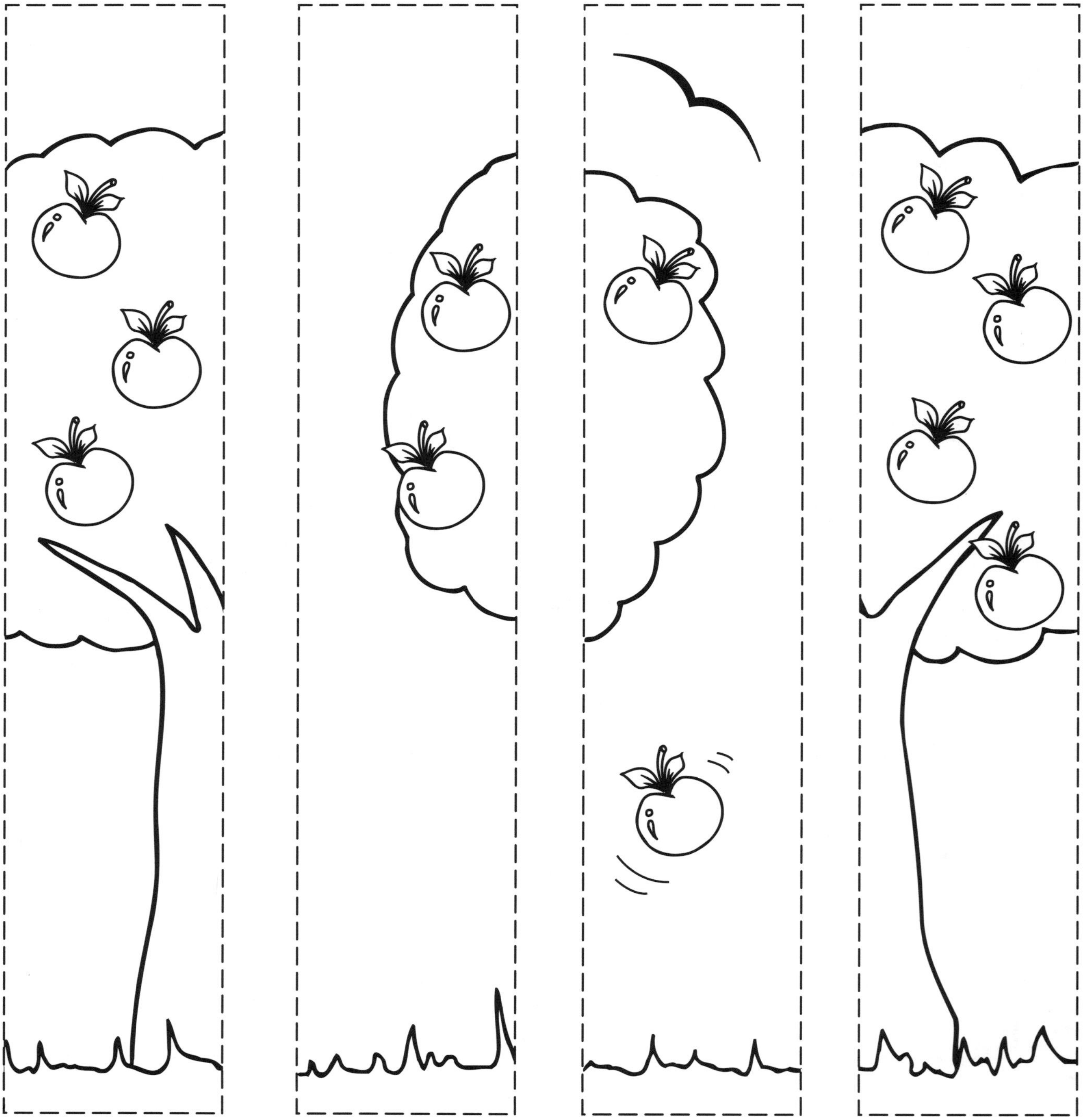

Name: ______________________________ Date: ___________________

1. color **2.** cut **3.** glue

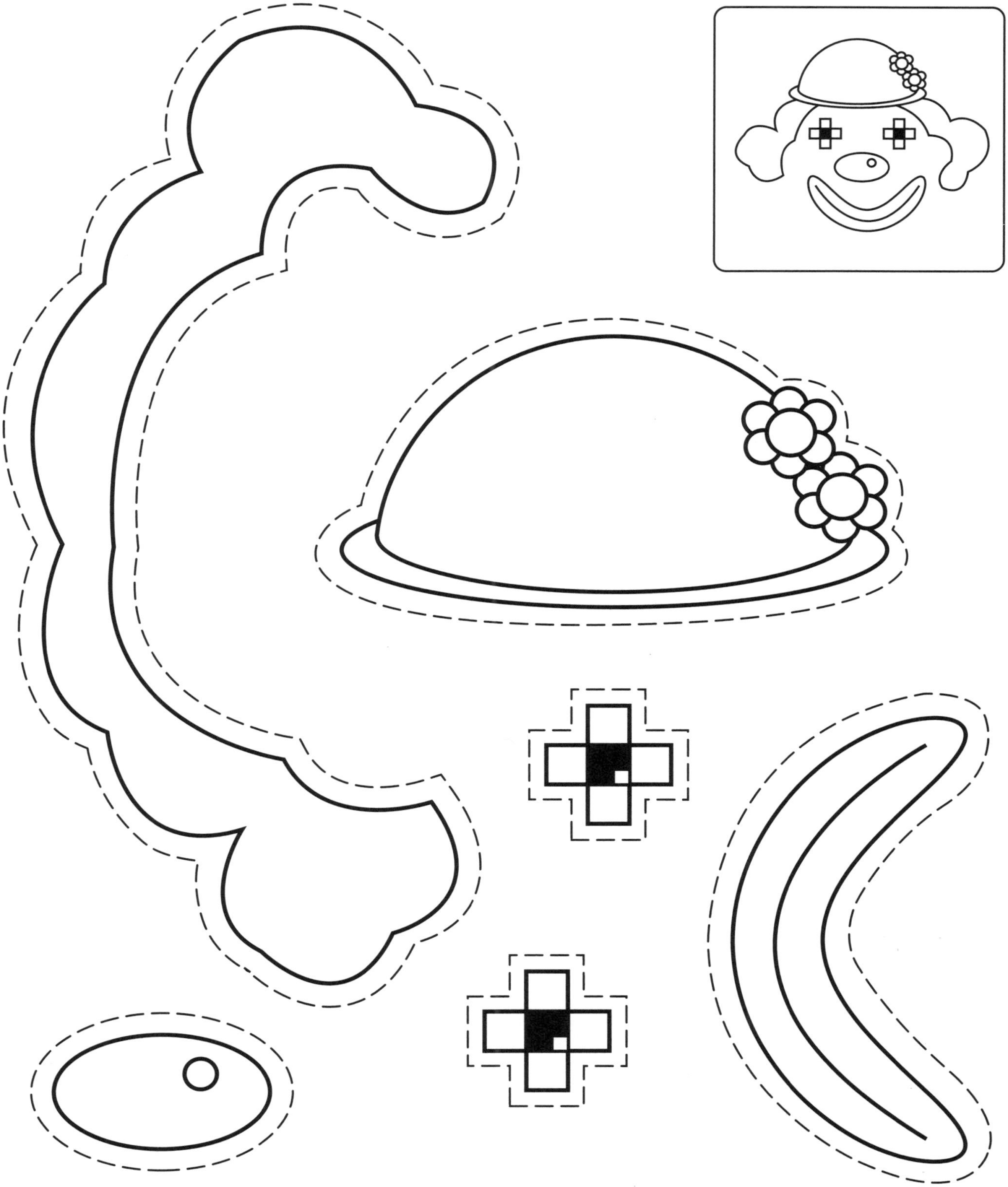

Name: ______________________ Date: ______________

1. 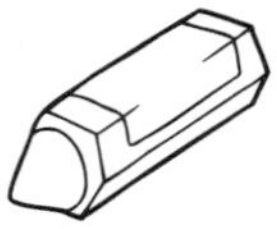 color 2. cut  3.  glue

www.worldteacherspress.com © World Teachers Press®

Name: ______________________ Date: ______________________

1. color **2.** cut **3.** glue

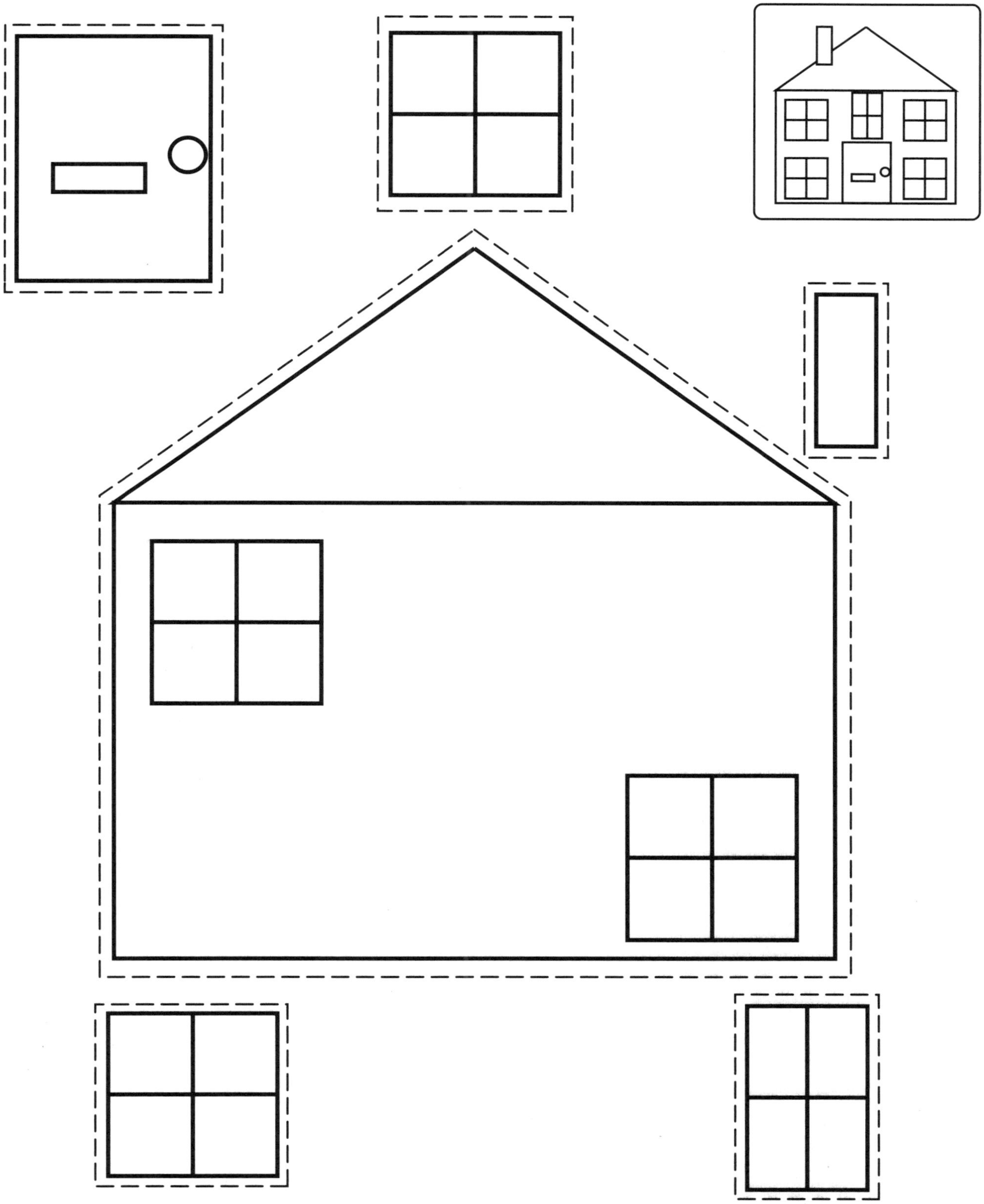

Name: ______________________________ Date: __________________

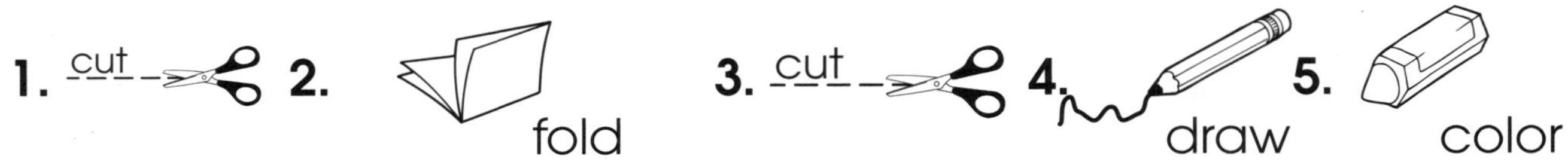

Name: ______________________________ Date: ____________________

Name: ______________________ Date: ______________

A sample page from the book, *Addition to Five*, also in the *Early Skills Series*.

1. 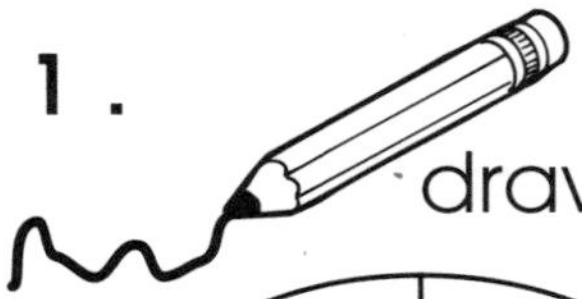 draw 2. 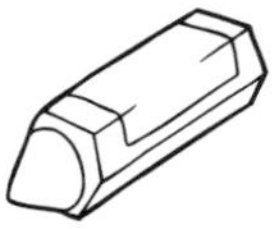 color 3.  count 4.  write

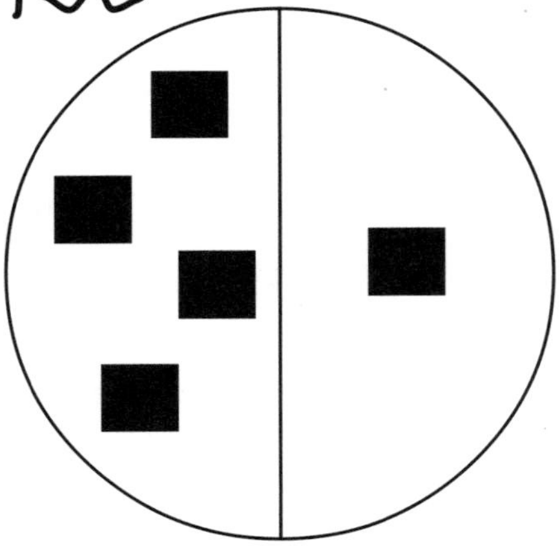

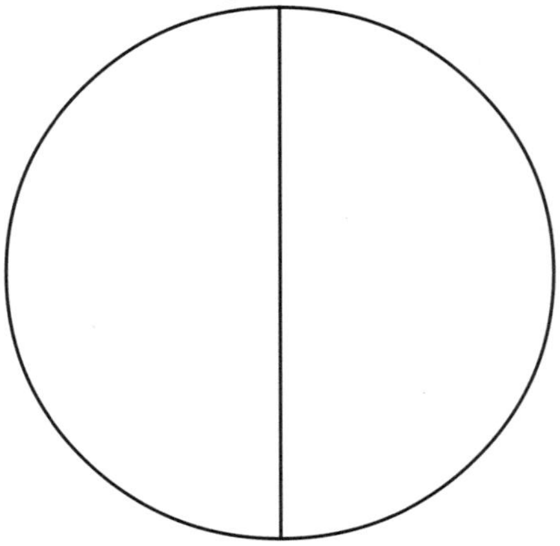

4 + 1 = ________ 2 + 3 = ________

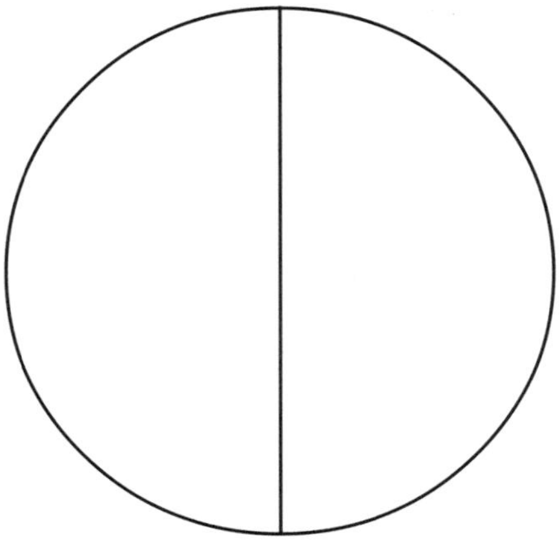

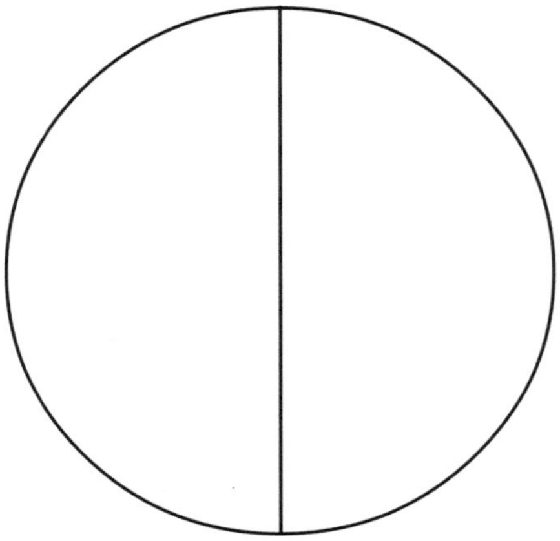

5 + 0 = ________ 2 + 2 = ________

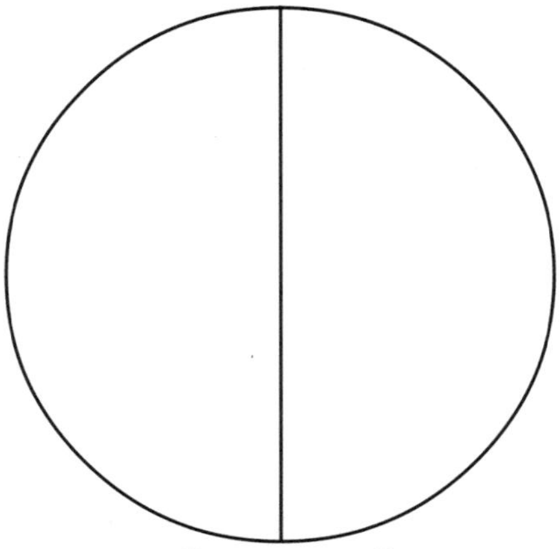

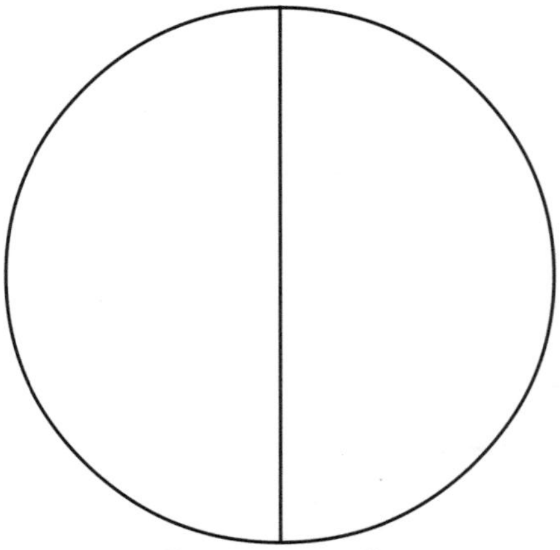

3 + 1 = ________ 1 + 2 = ________